Little Pebble™

KU-475-255

Habitats

All About
Grasslands

by Christina Mia Gardeski

raintree
a Capstone company — publishers for children

Raintree is an imprint of Capstone Global Library Limited, a company incorporated in England and Wales having its registered office at 264 Banbury Road, Oxford, OX2 7DY – Registered company number: 6695582

www.raintree.co.uk
myorders@raintree.co.uk

Text © Capstone Global Library Limited 2018
The moral rights of the proprietor have been asserted.

All rights reserved. No part of this publication may be reproduced in any form or by any means (including photocopying or storing it in any medium by electronic means and whether or not transiently or incidentally to some other use of this publication) without the written permission of the copyright owner, except in accordance with the provisions of the Copyright, Designs and Patents Act 1988 or under the terms of a licence issued by the Copyright Licensing Agency, Saffron House, 6–10 Kirby Street, London EC1N 8TS (www.cla.co.uk). Applications for the copyright owner's written permission should be addressed to the publisher.

Edited by Marissa Kirkman
Designed by Juliette Peters (cover) and Charmaine Whitman (interior)
Picture research by Eric Gohl
Production by Katy LaVigne
Originated by Capstone Global Library Limited
Printed and bound in India.

ISBN 978 1 4747 5266 4
21 20 19 18 17
10 9 8 7 6 5 4 3 2 1

British Library Cataloguing in Publication Data
A full catalogue record for this book is available from the British Library.

Acknowledgements
We would like to thank the following for permission to reproduce photographs: Shutterstock: AlinaMD, 7, BGSmith, 11, David Whitemyer, 5, dibrova, back cover, interior (grassland illustration), Dmussman, 20, Jeeri, cover, Oleksandr Fediuk, 19, Papa Bravo, 17 (top), Pedro Helder Pinheiro, 17 (bottom), pornpoj, 15, Ricardo Reitmeyer, 1, Robert L Kothenbeutel, 10, SnelsonStock, 6, tomtsya, 9, Volodymyr Burdiak, 13, Zeljko Radojko, 21

Every effort has been made to contact copyright holders of material reproduced in this book. Any omissions will be rectified in subsequent printings if notice is given to the publisher.

All the Internet addresses (URLs) given in this book were valid at the time of going to press. However, due to the dynamic nature of the Internet, some addresses may have changed, or sites may have changed or ceased to exist since publication. While the author and publisher regret any inconvenience this may cause readers, no responsibility for any such changes can be accepted by either the author or the publisher.

Contents

What are grasslands?

Grasslands are lands

of grass.

Animals live in the grass.

It is a busy habitat.

CHISLEHURS
020 8467 1318

− 4 MAR 2019

WITHDRAWN FROM
BROMLEY LIBRARIES

THE LONDON BOROUGH
www.bromley.gov.uk

Please return/renew this item
by the last date shown.
Books may also be renewed by
phone and Internet.

Bromley Libraries

30128 80338 608 8

The prairie

A prairie is flat.

It is hot in summer.

It is cold in winter.

winter

Deer eat the grass.

This makes it short.

Few trees grow.

Prairie dogs dig.

Hawks spy.

hawk

prairie dogs

The savannah

A savannah has hills.

It is warm all year.

13

The grass is tall.

Elephants graze.

Zebras run.

Lions hunt.

Fire!

A fire burns the grass.

The roots do not burn.

Rain falls.

Grass grows.

Grassland animals grow too.

Glossary

deer animal with hooves that runs fast and eats plants

graze eat grass

habitat home of a plant or animal

hawk large bird with sharp claws and a strong beak that hunts small animals

prairie grassland with hot summers and cold winters

prairie dog small animal that digs and lives in tunnels in the prairie

savannah grassland that is warm all year

zebra grassland animal with hooves and stripes that runs fast

Read more

Grassland Animals (Animals in Their Habitats), Sian Smith (Raintree, 2015)

Grassland Food Chains (Food Chains and Webs), Angela Royston (Raintree, 2015)

Living and Non-Living in the Grassland (Is It Living or Non-Living?), Rebecca Rissman (Raintree, 2014)

Websites

www.bbc.co.uk/nature/habitats/Temperate_grasslands,_savannas,_and_shrublands
Watch videos of grassland animals.

www.dkfindout.com/uk/animals-and-nature/habitats-and-ecosystems/land-habitats/
Find out about different habitats around the world.

Index